BUILT FOR SUCCESS

THE STORY OF

Nike

First published in the UK in 2011 by
Franklin Watts
338 Euston Road
London NW1 3BH

Franklin Watts Australia
Level 17/207 Kent Street
Sydney, NSW 2000

First published by Creative Education,
an imprint of The Creative Company.
Copyright © 2009 Creative Education.
International copyright reserved in all countries.
No part of this book may be reproduced in any
form without written permission from the publisher.

A CIP catalogue record for this book is available from the
British Library.

ISBN: 978 1 4451 0593 2
Dewey number: 338.7'68876

Printed in China

Franklin Watts is a division of
Hachette Children's Books,
an Hachette UK company.
www.hachette.co.uk

DESIGN AND PRODUCTION BY **ZENO DESIGN**

PHOTOGRAPHS BY Alamy (Laskowitz), Corbis (Bettmann,
Jonathan Ferrey, Wally McNamee, Franck Seguin/
TempSport), Getty Images (Andrew D. Bernstein/NBAE, Todd
Bigelow/Aurora, Tim Boyle, Clive Brunskill/Allsport, David
Cannon, MIKE CLARKE/AFP, Jonathan Ferrey, Mark Dadswell,
Jonathan Ferrey, FRANCK FIFE/AFP, Kevin Fleming, Nick
Laham, Alan Levenson//Time Life Pictures, Jasper Juinen,
Bob Martin/Allsport, Co Rentmeester//Time Life Pictures,
Ron Vesely), Oregon Archive.

BUILT FOR SUCCESS

THE STORY OF
Nike

W
FRANKLIN WATTS
LONDON • SYDNEY

AARON FRISCH

Dressed in brightly coloured Nike tights and top, Serena Williams tosses a tennis ball over her head and fires a scorching serve at her opponent. LeBron James streaks down the basketball court and soars to the rim for a slam dunk, his personalised Nike shoes propelling him a metre or more off the floor. Tiger Woods stands over a golf ball with a tiny curved logo on it then, flawlessly swinging a Nike iron, launches the ball 183 metres, narrowly missing the cup. No matter what the sport, Nike and its unmistakable 'Swoosh' logo are likely to be there. Today this giant of a corporation towers above all competitors in the sports clothing industry – however, Nike began nearly five decades ago with nothing but a young runner and an ambitious dream.

CHAPTER ONE

A blue-ribbon beginning

In the early 1960s, business graduate student Phil Knight was assigned a research paper on how he would create a new company. Born in Oregon, USA, Phil had run competitively in secondary school and university, so he settled on an idea of personal interest: how to design and sell track shoes.

After researching the industry Knight was left with an enterprising idea. He thought he really could start his own business by buying low-cost sports shoes made in Japan and selling them in America. "I had determined when I wrote that paper," Knight would later say, "that what I wanted to do with my life was to be the best track and field [athletics] shoe **distributor** in the United States."

At the time, American companies sold a lot of 'sneakers' – comfortable and inexpensive shoes that people wore for leisure activities. German manufacturers, especially Adidas, were known to make the best athletic shoes. Most serious athletes wore Adidas footwear, but Knight thought he could compete against the German outfitters by selling shoes for less.

In November 1962, Knight boarded a plane for Japan. There, he visited a sporting goods shop and saw a pair of running shoes with the brand name 'Tiger', manufactured by a company called Onitsuka. Knight took a train to the city

Phil Knight was aged 24 when he launched the athletic shoe company that would become Nike

of Kobe, where he met with executives of the company, telling them that he was a shoe **importer** from the United States. When asked the name of his company, which didn't yet exist, Knight said the first thing that popped into his head: Blue Ribbon Sports.

Knight's first order, five pairs of white-and-blue leather Tiger shoes, didn't arrive in the USA until more than a year later. Knight and Bill Bowerman, his former running coach at the University of Oregon, each contributed £310 ($500) to import more shoes. Bowerman agreed to **promote** the shoes to university athletes; Knight would handle everything else. Less than a year later, Knight had sold 1,300 pairs of running shoes out of the boot of his car at athletics meetings, supporting his fledgling business by working as an accountant.

In 1965, Knight met Jeff Johnson, a former running rival, at an athletics meeting and approached him about promoting Tiger shoes, offering an advance of £250 ($400) and an income based on **commission**. Johnson was not particularly interested but, in need of work, he agreed to sell them on a part-time basis. In 1966, he sold so many shoes that Knight hired him as the company's first full-time employee. Johnson inadvertently pushed Blue Ribbon Sports into the clothing business when he started handing out T-shirts with the Tiger name printed across the front to promote the shoes. The T-shirts became so popular that Johnson and Knight decided to sell them as well, and they opened their first retail shop along the busy Pico Boulevard in Santa Monica, California.

While Knight handled the business and Johnson handled the sales, Bill Bowerman provided much of the young company's inspiration. Bowerman was widely regarded as the finest running coach in America, and his running programme at the University of Oregon was legendary. His reputation grew in 1967 when he co-authored the book *Jogging: A Physical Fitness Program for All Ages*, which sold more than one million copies. The book explained how jogging could strengthen a person's heart and lungs, burn body fat and build endurance, and all that was required was a good pair of shoes. As a coach, Bowerman

Nike co-founder Bill Bowerman (right) coached athletics at the University of Oregon for 24 years

pushed his runners hard – "Nobody ever remembers number two" he liked to say – and was always looking for a competitive edge. He began tinkering with footwear designs, hoping to make Tiger shoes lighter and better-performing than anything else on the **market**.

In 1968, Bowerman designed a shoe that combined the best features of all the running shoes he had seen up to that point, including fuller 'heel to toe' cushioning. He showed it to executives at Onitsuka, who liked the design and manufactured the shoe just in time for the 1968 Summer Olympics in Mexico City. Blue Ribbon called it the Cortez, and it became one of the best-selling shoes that Bowerman and Knight would market as partners.

Bowerman next suggested to Onitsuka that it make a running shoe from nylon. The Japanese manufacturer elaborated on his idea, making a rubber-soled marathon shoe with a thin layer of foam sandwiched between two sheets of nylon. The shoe was lighter than anything made of leather or canvas. The Tiger Marathon, as it was called, changed the athletic shoe market forever.

Blue Ribbon Sports secured an **exclusive contract** to sell the Tiger Marathon and in 1969, revenues reached £250,000 ($400,000). One year later, the company earned £625,000 ($1 million) – but it also faced difficulties. While sales were good, Blue Ribbon's operating costs had soared. In addition, Onitsuka sometimes had difficulty shipping the larger orders on time and customers became annoyed with the delays. Facing these complications Knight and Bowerman soon decided to create their own brand.

"*If you have a body, you are an athlete.*"

BILL BOWERMAN, NIKE CO-FOUNDER

The 1968 Summer Olympics was Blue Ribbon Sports' first big chance to test its shoe designs

NIKE

THE MAN BEHIND NIKE

Philip Hampson Knight (far left) grew up in a suburb of Portland, Oregon, in the USA. Known to his childhood friends as 'Buck', he enjoyed sport but wasn't big enough to excel at American football or basketball. As a teenager, he took up running instead. When he enrolled at the University of Oregon, Knight joined the athletics team, coached by a passionate running enthusiast called Bill Bowerman. The coach would later help Knight start the Blue Ribbon Sports company. Knight seemed an unlikely leader to build up a multi-billion-dollar company – he was quiet and hated speaking in public ("I still get real nervous when I go in front of more than two people," he said in 2005) – but he had a knack for surrounding himself with talented executives. By 2010, Knight remained company chairman and his stake in Nike made him one of the wealthiest men in America, with a net worth of about £7.9 billion ($12.7 billion).

CHAPTER TWO

A company with sole

In 1971, Blue Ribbon Sports' co-founders designed a new shoe but they needed cash to manufacture it. To generate the necessary funds they decided to sell part of the company. By autumn 1971, **investors** owned about 35 per cent of Blue Ribbon Sports.

Buoyed by the added funds, the partners were soon promoting a new line of shoes they called Nike. (The name, a reference to the Greek goddess of victory, came to Jeff Johnson in a dream and replaced Phil Knight's original choice, 'Dimension 6'.)

In June 1971, Blue Ribbon's first shoes bearing the Nike name and its unique 'Swoosh' logo went on sale. Unfortunately there was a major glitch. The shoes were made in the warm climate of Mexico and no one had tested them in the cold weather of the northern United States. The soles cracked and the shoes had to be sold at a reduced price. The company had manufactured 10,000 pairs and almost all were sold for a mere £5 ($7.95).

In October of that year, Knight flew to Japan with a new **line of credit** from a Japanese trading company called Nissho Iwai. With this credit line Knight ordered 6,000 pairs of the popular Tiger Cortez, but now he requested that Onitsuka put the Nike logo on every pair. On the same trip, he purchased basketball and wrestling shoes, as well as casual street shoes, from other Japanese manufacturers.

Nike's distinctive – and now globally recognised – 'Swoosh' logo was first introduced in 1971

In the early 1970s, as Blue Ribbons's operations and staff grew, Knight sought out employees with a flair for creative thinking and a nonconformist attitude. He enjoyed hearing his employees talk about sport and loud arguments were a common – and even encouraged – part of meetings at the Nike workplace. One observer who visited the company's offices remarked, "Nike is like high school [secondary school], only with money."

In 1972, the US Men's Track and Field Olympic Trials were held in Eugene, Oregon, and athletes from all over America came to compete for a chance to make the Olympic team. The event was significant to Nike for two reasons. Firstly, a fiery runner from the University of Oregon called Steve Prefontaine, soon to become one of the public faces of the Nike name, emerged as a star. The event also shone a spotlight on Blue Ribbon Sports, as the company's shoes could be seen on the feet of many top athletes. Nike shoes were not low-priced the way the first Tiger shoes were, but athletes appreciated the high quality of design and manufacture.

During the same year, Bowerman had a shoe design epiphany. One day, he poured some liquid **latex** into his wife's hot waffle iron. The result was a ruined waffle iron and a solid piece of latex with a square pattern. Bowerman showed the moulded sample to Knight, who liked the idea of a textured, latex sole that would give runners and American football players better **traction** while reducing shoe weight. The Waffle outsole was born, and the Waffle Trainer shoe would be unveiled to the public in 1974.

In 1972, Blue Ribbon Sports sold 250,000 pairs of running shoes and 50,000 pairs of basketball shoes. Business was booming but the company had a problem. When Onitsuka learned that Blue Ribbon was selling Japanese-made shoes other than Tigers, it decided to find other US distributors. Knight filed a lawsuit against Onitsuka in 1973, charging that the manufacturer had broken its contract. Onitsuka counter-sued, alleging that Blue Ribbon had used the Tiger **trademark** illegally to push the sales of Nike shoes. At the end of the bitter

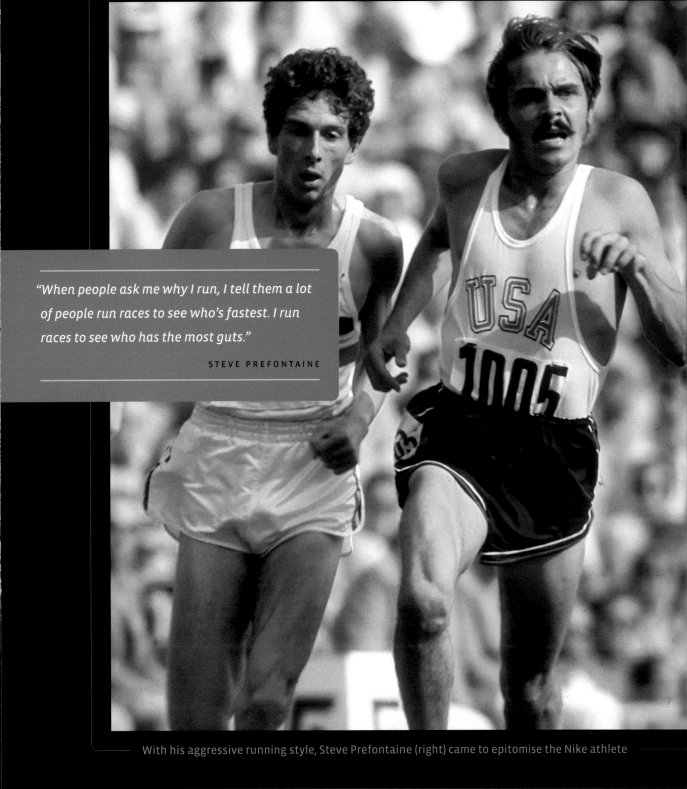

> "When people ask me why I run, I tell them a lot of people run races to see who's fastest. I run races to see who has the most guts."
>
> STEVE PREFONTAINE

With his aggressive running style, Steve Prefontaine (right) came to epitomise the Nike athlete

NIKE

dispute, a judge allowed both Blue Ribbon Sports and Onitsuka to sell the shoe designs they had worked on together. Only Blue Ribbon, however, could use the model names such as Cortez.

Blue Ribbon Sports had lost its main Japanese supply line, but Knight was confident he could continue to build up the company, partly through **endorsements**. Steve Prefontaine became Nike's first endorser when Knight and Bowerman agreed in 1973 to pay for his training if he wore their shoes and shorts. Prefontaine was exactly what Nike aspired to represent. With his wild, flowing hair, he cut a unique and instantly recognisable image, and he ran with a rare passion and determination, pushing through pain and fatigue that would have stopped most runners.

'Pre' won several national university championships in the early 1970s and was poised for international stardom. However, his life and career were cut short when he was killed in a car accident in 1975. At the time of his death, the 24-year-old held seven US track records. Pre was gone but he would become a legend and a lasting influence at Nike. Not only had his commitment to the brand established Nike as a legitimate sports brand, but his fiery spirit had helped to shape Nike's mission: "To bring inspiration and **innovation** to every athlete in the world."

By summer 1975, Blue Ribbon Sports had signed several top National Basketball Association (NBA) players, including Elvin Hayes and Spencer Haywood, to endorsement deals. Each player received £1,250 ($2,000) a year and a small **royalty** from profits on Nike basketball shoes. The cost of signing such big-name players to endorsement contracts rose quickly; within a few years, companies would be paying NBA players up to £6,250 ($10,000) to wear their shoes. The world of sport was expanding quickly and the money involved was expanding with it.

Nike sponsors the annual Prefontaine Classic, a premier athletics meeting held at the University of Oregon in the USA

SWOOSH – THE NIKE LOGO

In 1970, the new Nike line of shoes needed a logo, a symbol that people would associate with the brand. Blue Ribbon Sports executives wanted something that suggested movement and speed and would also set them apart from other shoe companies. Adidas, for example, had three stripes on the arch of its shoes while Puma had a stripe that ran along the sides. Knight asked Carolyn Davidson, an art student he knew, to come up with several designs. After reviewing her sketches Knight and his partners finally decided on a logo that resembled a rounded tick. "I don't love it," Knight admitted, "but maybe it will grow on me." The logo did grow on him. Over time, the symbol (for which Davidson charged £22 or $35) became known as the "Swoosh" – it is today one of the most recognisable trademarks in the world.

CHAPTER THREE

Jordan and beyond

In the late 1970s, Blue Ribbon Sports made great strides in shoe design. In 1977, Frank Rudy – former engineer with space agency NASA – came up with an idea to reduce the shock of impact when running and jumping on hard pavements. He suggested placing pockets of air inside the shoe's sole to cushion the foot.

The first shoes did not hold up well, the air pockets deflating after a hard jog, but Knight liked the idea. He added Frank Rudy to the Blue Ribbon payroll and told him to keep experimenting.

Knight and his team introduced a running shoe called the Tailwind in 1979, just after the company name was officially changed to Nike. The Tailwind was very light and the sole contained tiny sacs filled with gas – a cushioning system that came to be known as Nike Air. Athletes could run, jump and play as hard as they wanted, with less fear of injury, and their shoes would spring back to their original shape.

In 1980, Nike pulled in £168 million ($269 million) and reached a major milestone by replacing Adidas as the most popular athletic shoe in the USA. Amidst this growth Nike began to sell **stock** to the public. In Blue Ribbon's earliest years, friends and family members had contributed £3,000 ($5,000) each when Knight and Bowerman needed money to keep the company going. By the early 1980s, those £3,000 ($5,000) investments had skyrocketed to a value of £1.87 million ($3 million) each.

The Air sole technology developed by Nike in the late 1970s is still used in many of the company's shoes

Nike shoes were well-represented at the 1980 Olympic Trials, and university baseball and American football programmes and coaches were now on the Nike payroll as well, being decked out in team uniforms and shoes bearing Nike's **signature** Swoosh. But it was in the professional ranks that the company spent the most money expanding the Nike name. In 1978, Nike had signed a young tennis player called John McEnroe for £62,500 ($100,000). McEnroe was the top tennis money-maker of the day – even when he wasn't winning he received considerable media attention due to his flamboyant personality and frequent on-court temper tantrums. In 1981, long-distance runner Alberto Salazar gave Nike free publicity when he set a world marathon record wearing Nikes. By then, Nike's inventory included more than 200 kinds of shoes.

By the mid-1980s, Nike had decided not to pay large numbers of athletes to endorse its shoes; instead, it would entice a small number – the most elite – with huge contracts. In 1984, Nike signed its first megastar, basketball sensation Michael Jordan. When Jordan left university for the NBA, the Chicago Bulls signed him to a five-year, £1.87-million ($3-million) contract. Nike, confident that it was getting a rare marketing force and a player who would make television news highlights on a nightly basis, signed the young man to a five-year, £1.5-million ($2.5-million) deal and created his own personal shoe: the Air Jordan, a reference both to the shoes' cushioning technology and the way Jordan so effortlessly leapt through the air.

When Jordan took to the court for the first time wearing his special red-and-black shoes, the NBA fined the Bulls £625 ($1,000) for violating the league's uniform dress code. Nike cleverly seized on the fine as a publicity opportunity, producing a television advert that showed Jordan bouncing a ball as a voice said: "On September 15, Nike created a revolutionary new basketball shoe. On October 18, the NBA threw them out of the game. Fortunately the NBA can't keep you from wearing them. Air Jordans from Nike."

Tennis star John McEnroe was just 19 years old when he signed an endorsement deal with Nike in 1978

As Jordan forged a legacy as the greatest basketball player of all time, Nike grew exponentially. Throughout the 1980s (and 1990s), in every year except 1987, Nike shoes would be the top-selling athletic footwear in the world. The 1987 stumble was due largely to Nike's failure to recognise the newest trend in fitness, a low-impact type of exercise called aerobics. The company fell into second place that year behind Reebok, whose aerobics shoes sold well. The defeat cast light onto a market that Nike had previously overlooked; up until that time, the vast majority of the company's products and advertisements had been aimed at men. Reebok's surge made it clear that female sportspeople represented an audience that needed much greater attention.

As Nike responded with expanded footwear and clothing lines for women, it also unveiled a new kind of shoe: the cross-trainer. These shoes were more ruggedly built than running shoes and were more versatile, designed not only for running but for weightlifting or aerobics as well. In 1989, Nike found the perfect spokesman for its cross-trainers: Bo Jackson. A remarkably fast and powerful athlete, Jackson had starred as a baseball outfielder and an American football running back (offensive player) at Auburn University in Alabama, USA. He decided to turn professional in baseball in 1986, then went pro in American football in 1987.

Nike signed Jackson to pitch a shoe called the Air Trainer, creating a wildly successful **ad campaign** featuring the slogan 'Bo Knows' and entertaining commercials that showed Jackson doing everything from playing tennis to running **luge**. The idea was that Nike's trainers were the perfect choice for almost any sport, just like Bo. Thanks largely to such successful endorsement decisions, in 1993 *Sporting News* magazine called Phil Knight 'the most powerful man in sport'.

While his pro American football career lasted only four seasons, Bo Jackson was a huge star for Nike

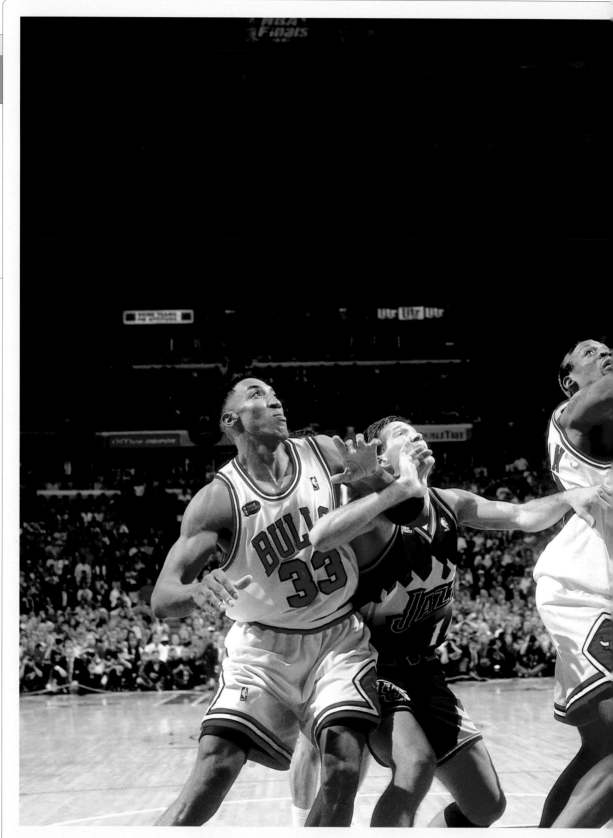

AIR JORDAN

In 1984, Michael Jordan left the University of North Carolina before finishing his degree to join the Chicago Bulls in the NBA. Nike executives desperately wanted the high-flying young star to wear their shoes but Jordan actually preferred Adidas, having worn them throughout secondary school and university. In the end, Nike made him an offer he couldn't turn down: £1.5 million ($2.5 million) over five years and his own line of Nike basketball shoes, called Air Jordans. Air Jordans, like Jordan himself, were an instant sensation. In 1985, customers bought £80 million ($130 million) worth of the shoes. Jordan went on to play in the NBA for 15 seasons and Air Jordans – which were re-designed year after year – remained a high-selling product years after he retired. In 2011, Nike released the newest model, the £125 ($200) Air Jordan 2011 Men's Basketball Shoe. "There's Michael Jordan," NBA star Magic Johnson once said, "and then there is the rest of us."

CHAPTER FOUR

Just do it

In 1991, Nike became the first sports and fitness company ever to earn more than £1.87 billion ($3 billion) in a year. Then, from 1995 to 1997, it grew at an astonishing rate. By the end of the 1997 **fiscal year**, the company had sold more than £5.6 billion ($9 billion) in shoes, clothing and sports equipment.

Big-name endorsements continued to be responsible for much of this growth and popularity. In 1996, more than a decade after signing Michael Jordan, Nike signed another young sporting icon: golfer Tiger Woods. Woods, a man of mixed race in a game that had long been considered a 'white sport', piqued the interest of a new generation of golfers with his spectacular drives and unshakeable focus. Knight paid £25 million ($40 million) for the 20-year-old's endorsement; in 2000, after Woods had won nearly 20 professional tournaments and Nike Golf had become an official brand, the contract would be reworked to a massive £65 million ($105 million).

Nike built new product lines and marketing campaigns around Woods and other elite sportspeople such as baseball star Derek Jeter, underscoring an attitude that was distinctly Nike: hardworking, competitive, tough… and fashionable. Many Nike advertisements also featured less-famous athletes – and even ordinary people – with the 'Just Do It' slogan to emphasise that anyone could be an athlete. All it

Tiger Woods' £65-million Nike contract was the largest endorsement deal ever signed by a sportsperson

took was sweat and dedication. In the mid-1990s, Nike produced a number of adverts aimed exclusively at female athletes; one Nike T-shirt bore the slogan 'I am woman, watch me score'.

By the late 1990s, Nike was the undisputed king of the sports clothing industry. But the company began to find that its position left it exposed to criticism. Nike prided itself on aggressive advertising but some critics saw the company's tactics as ruthless and even tacky. For the 1996 Olympics, for example, Nike won the bidding rights to be the official outfitter of the US Track and Field Team and soon revealed tracksuits that had Swooshes instead of stars in the American flag. The alteration triggered loud complaints and the uniforms were changed. Nike also created controversy with its hyper-competitive Olympic slogan "You Don't Win Silver – You Lose Gold".

In 1998, Nike seemed to hit a wall as its overall revenues dropped off by 8 per cent. Sales in the Asian market, a region keen on Nike products in the past, fell sharply. Nike sold 50 per cent of trainers purchased worldwide in 1998 but that was a lower percentage than the company had enjoyed the year before. The problem, Knight believed, was that Nike had become too big too fast and thus inefficient. To remedy the problem 1,200 employees were **made redundant** and operating costs were reduced by almost £125 million ($200 million).

Yet perhaps the most damaging blow Nike took in the late 1990s was the public accusation that the company mistreated its overseas employees. Nike had several hundred factories worldwide by then, mostly in Asia where operating costs were lower. News reports revealed that many of these factories were 'sweatshops' which paid their workers below-scale wages; for example, in 1996 in Indonesia, a country that manufactured 70 million pairs of shoes a year, thousands of workers were paid less than £1.50 ($2.50) a day. Overseas managers sometimes hired employees as young as age 14 and it was also brought to light that many Nike factories used dangerous chemicals in the manufacturing process without installing proper equipment to improve employee safety.

As an official outfitter and pioneer in performance wear, Nike has been prominently represented in recent Olympics

Faced with these serious charges Knight acted quickly to minimise the damage. Issuing an equally public response he pledged in 1998 to change company policies to ensure that Nike employees at overseas factories would be treated fairly, that the company would establish a minimum hiring age in its factories, and that Nike would tighten air-quality standards at the sites. "These moves do more than just set industry standards," he said. "They reflect who we are as a company."

In the first few years of the 21st century, Nike slowly recovered from the 1998 setback. By 2002, the company's revenues had crept up to $6.2 billion ($9.9 billion). A £3,000 ($5,000) share from Blue Ribbon Sports' early days was now worth more than £18.7 million ($30 million). During these years most of the company's growth occurred outside the USA. Knight had long dreamt of turning Nike into a truly global corporation and rising sales in Europe, Asia and South America were proof of the company's ever-expanding reach. Since 1990, Nike had been opening superstores called Niketowns throughout the USA and the rest of the world. The shops, essentially enormous showrooms, sold a vast range of company products, including virtually every current model of Nike trainer. They also featured basketball courts and giant statues of sporting heroes. By 2007, there were Niketowns doing brisk business in such foreign locations as London and Hong Kong.

Nike also addressed the stagnant growth of the late 1990s by tapping into new corners of the sporting world. The company expanded its All Conditions Gear (ACG) product line designed for outdoor pursuits such as hiking, kayaking and biking. In 1994, Nike had bought into ice hockey in a large way by acquiring Bauer, a leading manufacturer of ice hockey equipment and clothing. In 2002, the company entered the world of skateboarding, surfing and snowboarding by making the Hurley International company a **subsidiary**, thereby adding clothing for these 'alternative' sports to the Nike family.

NEVER UNDERESTIMATE THE POWER OF PLAY.

Rx FOR

AIR VAPOR CONTROL

GET FASTER IN THE

ZOOM VAPOR TRAINER

> "From Bowerman's Waffle Trainer to the Tour Accuracy golf ball, we make every effort to take consumers where they want to go before they realise they want to go there."
>
> PHIL KNIGHT

Niketowns throughout the world average more than 2,700 square metres (30,000 sq ft) per shop.

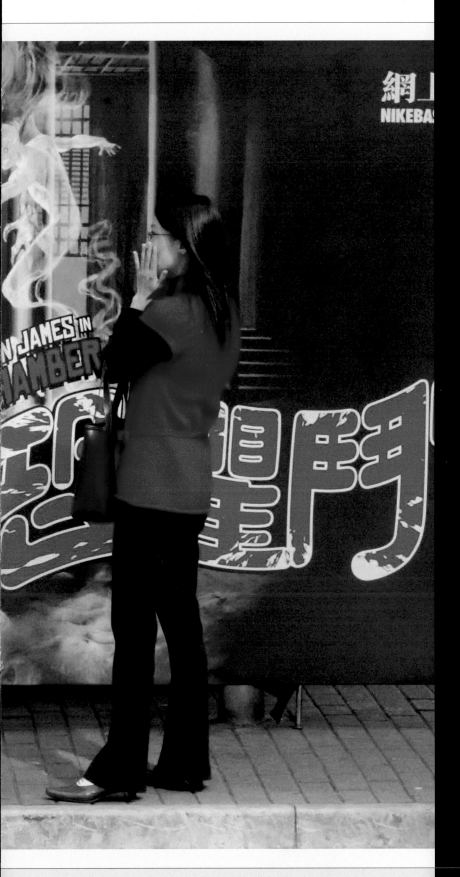

NIKE WORLDWIDE

Although Nike was born in the USA, the company didn't turn into a true giant until it started branching out into foreign countries. The company entered its first foreign market, Canada, in 1972 and expanded operations to Australia in 1974. In 1977, Nike lined up distributorships in Asia and did the same in South America in 1978. In the first years of the 21st century, sales of footwear and clothing to customers in foreign markets made up an increasingly larger share of Nike's revenues, and by 2011, the company was selling its products in more than 170 countries. The statistics below show the global distribution of Nike's earnings during the 2010 fiscal year.

TOTAL REVENUE:	£10.3 billion ($16.5 billion)
North America:	£4.2 billion ($6.7 billion)
Europe:	£3.1 billion ($5 billion)
Greater China and Japan:	£1.6 billion ($2.6 billion)
Other:	£1.4 billion ($2.2 billion)

Source: *2010 Nike Annual Report*

Taking on the world

As Nike's offerings grew, so did its sports technology innovations. In 2000, Nike took its Air system to another level with Nike Shox, a sole technology that used a springy, resilient foam for cushioning. The same year, the company unveiled a ground-breaking line of form-fitting bodysuits.

Given such names as the Swift Suit and Swift Spin, they were the result of years of research and testing in wind tunnels. By carefully combining a range of lightweight, elastic fibres Nike's design team created a 'second skin' that made athletes' bodies more **aerodynamic**. Different suits were made for sprinters, speed skaters, swimmers, cyclists and other sportspeople whose goal was to go as fast as possible. In the years that followed, the suits could be seen on such Olympic heroes as Australian sprinter Cathy Freeman and US speed skater Apolo Anton Ohno.

In 2003, Nike made big headlines twice. Firstly, it purchased Converse for £190 million ($305 million). Converse was a shoe company with a 95-year history and although it had never been a serious rival to Nike, it was a popular brand known for its 'old school' canvas basketball shoes. Then, only weeks later, Nike signed basketball phenomenon LeBron James to a seven-year, £56-million ($90-million) endorsement deal. Although James was only 18 years old (and about to jump

Speed skater Apolo Anton Ohno won two Olympic medals in 2002 wearing Nike's Swift Skin suit

straight from secondary school into the NBA), he was widely seen as the "next Michael Jordan" – many industry experts thought he might one day become the first billion-dollar athlete in the world through his basketball and endorsement contracts. "Nike is the right fit and has the right product for me," said 'King James', who stands 2.03 m (6 ft 8 in) in height. James LeBron was given his own signature Nike collection.

Nike was again scoring high but there were stumbles along the way. In 2004, Knight stepped down as the company's chief executive officer (CEO) and handed the reins to William Perez, formerly the CEO of SC Johnson & Son, a household products company. But Perez's tenure was short. The new CEO wanted to break away from Nike's tradition of spending big money on advertising and he and Knight, now company chairman, soon clashed. By early 2006, Perez would be asked to resign and would be replaced by Nike executive Mark Parker.

A more public bump in the road emerged in 2006 when Adidas, Nike's long-time rival, purchased Reebok. Suddenly Nike's two most significant challengers were turned into a single, powerful competitor. Although Nike made nearly £9.3 billion ($15 billion) in 2006, football powerhouse Adidas brought in a formidable £5.9 billion ($9.5 billion) and was determined to continue narrowing the gap. Nike had largely ignored football – the most popular sport in the world outside of the USA – during its first four decades but that would change. The company had capitalised on the jogging boom of the 1970s, the basketball heyday of the 1980s and the cross-training craze of the 1990s. Now, it resolved to make deep inroads into the world of football.

In 2006, Nike took a major step in that direction by signing Brazilian star Ronaldinho, the best football player in the world, to his own signature collection. (Two years earlier, Nike had signed American Freddy Adu, a 14-year-old football whiz, to a £625,000 ($1-million) contract.) Nike also spent more than £62.5 million ($100 million) on advertising during the 2006 World Cup tournament, while Adidas spent close to £125 million ($200 million). Adidas had built its name on

The long-standing and intense rivalry between Nike and Adidas is most evident today on football pitches

the sport of football and it made clear the fact that Nike was going to face a tough fight to claim that throne. "Soccer [football] is the lifeblood and the backbone of our brand," said Adidas executive Erich Stamminger. "It's very, very emotional for us."

By 2010, Nike employed about 34,000 people and intended to become even bigger. To do this, the company planned to grow in all phases, but especially to expand operations in countries such as Russia, India and Brazil, each of which, Nike believed, could become a billion-dollar market. In early 2011, however, affected by the global economic downturn, the company experienced a fall in profits due to higher production costs. Mark Parker remained optimistic, pointing out Nike's edge as innovators: "Whatever may be unknown in the global economy, you can be absolutely certain that we'll continue to invest in our single biggest competitive advantage: our fixation on innovation that benefits consumers and shareholders."

Nike – the little shoe distributor from Oregon that grew to span the world as a sports clothing empire – has long had more than its share of detractors. Nike loyalists admire the innovation, vision and competitive spirit that have made the company famous, while critics denounce the high-priced 'premium product' philosophy which they say makes Nike big money while ignoring or mistreating people on low incomes. But what no one can dispute is that the company with the Swoosh is today king in the world of sport – and it plans to stay in power for a very long time.

"There's no way either one would even approach Nike, much less overtake them, on their own. This new, combined entity has a chance to make a run. Now, it's game on."

ADVERTISING EXECUTIVE JON HICKEY
ON THE 2006 MERGER OF ADIDAS AND REEBOK

In revenues, athletes and advertisements, Nike today intends to remain the biggest and the best

In 2007, *Fortune* magazine ranked
Nike at number 69 on its list of '100
Best Companies to Work For'. In
giving the company such praise, the
magazine stressed Nike's unique
workplace atmosphere and facilities:
"The Oregon campus is a sporting
paradise with tennis courts, indoor
and outdoor tracks, soccer [football]
fields, running trails, two sports
centres and an 11-lane pool used
for swimming, scuba and kayaking
lessons." Indeed, Nike's 'World
Campus' headquarters, which opened
in Beaverton, Oregon, in 1990
represents rare success and a singular
vision. The facility, which originally
covered 30 hectares (74 acres) and
has since more than doubled in size
is surrounded by woods and features
running paths, lakes and high-tech
fitness centres. Buildings on the
sprawling campus are named after
famous 'Nike athletes' such as tennis
great John McEnroe, basketball
legend Michael Jordan and cycling
hero Lance Armstrong, and the
company issues bonuses to employees
who cycle to work rather than drive

GLOSSARY

ad campaign a series of advertisements with a common theme

aerodynamic able to move through air or water with very little resistance

commission money paid to salespeople by their employer as a percentage of their sales

distributor an individual or company that sells and delivers another company's product to retail shops

endorsements business deals in which a well-known person is paid to express approval of a product

exclusive contract an agreement between two parties in which they promise to do business only with each other in a given market

fiscal year a 12-month schedule by which a company keeps records of its earnings; it differs by company and usually does not correspond to the calendar year

importer someone who buys products in a foreign country in order to sell them in his or her own country

innovation a new idea or way of doing something

investors people who put money into a company; their money grows if the company is financially successful

latex a substance found in various plants that is used to make rubber and some plastics

line of credit an agreement to lend money, or supply credit, to an individual or company

luge a sport in which a person rides a small sledge down a chute, lying flat on his or her back, trying to complete the 'run' in the fastest time possible

made redundant dismissed (as employees) not because of poor individual performance but because a company is trying to save money

market a geographic region or segment of the population to which companies try to sell goods; for example, the European market, the youth market or the world market

promote to encourage the use of a product amongst consumers by explaining its benefits

royalty a share of a product's proceeds paid to someone in exchange for an endorsement or other valuable contribution

signature something that is unique to a certain person and is often given distinctive or easily recognisable features

stock shared ownership in a company by many people who buy shares, or portions, of stock, hoping the company will make a profit and the stock value will increase

subsidiary a company that retains its own name but is entirely controlled by another company

traction the ability of an object to grip a surface; the texture of a shoe's sole, for example, can prevent a runner slipping

trademark a symbol or name that belongs legally and exclusively to one company; it may also refer to something that is unique about a company

1962 Phil Knight and his partner Bill Bowerman form Blue Ribbon Sports to distribute Japanese athletic shoes.

1965 Knight approaches Jeff Johnson to sell shoes for Blue Ribbon Sports. Johnson eventually starts selling T-shirts as well.

1967 Bowerman's best-selling book *Jogging* is published.

1971 Blue Ribbon launches its Nike shoe.

1973 Steve Prefontaine becomes Nike's first endorser.

1974 Waffle Trainer shoe launched.

1979 Blue Ribbon Sports officially changes its name to Nike.

1980 Nike takes over from Adidas as the USA's most popular athletic shoe.

1984 Nike signs basketball megastar Michael Jordan.

1989 Nike introduces the cross-trainer

1991 Nike sales top $3 billion.

Late 1990s Nike hit by allegations of sweatshop labour.

2000 Nike introduces form-fitting bodysuits.

2003 Nike buys sports shoe manufacturer Converse.

2006 Nike signs Brazilian football superstar Ronaldinho.

2010 Nike's plans to expand into India, Russia and Brazil are hit by the global economic downturn.

INDEX